VCU The A Game

VCU The A Game

Nine Steps to Better Grades

by Kenneth J. Sufka, Ph. D.

SECOND EDITION

THE NAUTILUS PUBLISHING COMPANY
OXFORD, MISSISSIPPI

Front cover design by Matthew Desmond, www.madtype.com

Permissions
Page 44: from Nickerson and Adams (1979), "Long-term memory for a common object." *Cognitive Psychology*, 11, 287-307. Reprinted with permission from Elsevier.
Page 52: from Novak, J. D. & A. J. Cañas, *The Theory Underlying Concept Maps and How to Construct and Use Them*, Technical Report IHMC CmapTools 2006-01 Rev 01-2008, Florida Institute for Human and Machine Cognition, 2008. Used with permission.

For bulk orders and educational discounts, contact:
The Nautilus Publishing Company
426 South Lamar Blvd, Suite 16, Oxford, MS 38655
www.nautiluspublishing.com
662-513-0159 • info@nautiluspublishing.com

Sufka, Kenneth J. (1960-   )
VCU The A Game: Nine Steps to Better Grades —2nd ed. ISBN # 978-1-94945503-8

The author and publisher welcome feedback. To offer suggestions or criticism, visit *www.TheAGameBook.com*

PRINTED IN THE U.S.

Contents

Introduction

During my nearly thirty years as a college professor, hundreds of students have stopped by my office to talk about their dismal class performances.

Many of my first-year college students insist they performed well in high school. But those same students claim my general psychology course is a challenge. The study skills that worked so well for them in high school no longer seem to work for college-level courses.

In my discussions with these students, I have discovered what contributes to poor exam performance: **a set of horrible habits and study strategies**. Some are merely ineffective. Others actually interfere with what students have learned. In more than one instance, these deadly habits lead to scores below chance-level performance on my exams. In posting grades, I've even added a new letter grade below F — EF for the Epic Fail!

But I have great news. In all of those years of helping students rid themselves of these tendencies, I have discovered what is necessary for students to become strategic learners and earn excellent grades.

I've seen success stories in every class, every semester. One student named Stephanie failed her first biopsychology test. She stopped by to discuss how she might better prepare for the next one. I went through my diagnostic checklist and gave her my list of strategic learning strategies sprinkled with a few real-world examples. On the second exam she scored an A. It was a low A but, nevertheless, an A.

I was floored. I sent her a congratulatory note and asked what she had done to prepare for the exam. She said, "I did everything you suggested."

Another student, Marcus, failed his first test. He scored a D on the second, a C on the third, a B on the fourth, and an A on the fifth. Marcus just took a little longer than Stephanie to bring his A game into the classroom.

Even good students can benefit. A third student, Reagan,

earned an A in my general psychology class but started my biopsychology class with a B- and C- on her first two exams. She then stopped by my office and learned she had not used **all** of *The A Game* study habits and strategies. She went on to earn an A on the third test and the highest test scores on the last two exams. The great news is that those three exam scores brought her final grade to an A after sitting on a C grade early in the term!

Each of the rules in this book is designed to make you a more strategic learner. The rules are intended **to rid you of useless and harmful learning habits and strategies** and to replace those with evidenced-based habits and strategies (see Dunlosky, et al., 2013 for an excellent review) that work to bring your A game into the classroom. **These habits and strategies work.** Master some and you'll find yourself with better grades. Master all of them and you will find yourself not only with better grades, but also with more free time. That's right. More free time and better grades.

Are you ready to get your A game on? Let's get started.

Kenneth J. Sufka, Ph.D.

Rule

Go To Class
— Always

A

Several years ago, a first-year student from Texas in my general psychology class called me. I could tell, immediately, she was in some sort of trouble. She said she was concerned with her grades and needed to speak with me as soon as possible.

At this point in the semester, I had already given two of five exams, and the third was just days away. I pulled the course records to see how big a hole she'd dug for herself. I scrolled through my list until I found her scores. She was in trouble, all right. She had no scores.

She had missed the first and the second exam.

I asked what was going on and she confessed to having not attended any of my classes since the first day.

"Why?" I asked, "Do you have some chronic illness? Family troubles at home?"

She said it was because I did not have an attendance policy. This is true; I neither give points for attendance nor take them away for non-attendance. "So," I asked, "how is my attendance policy working out for you?"

Sheepishly, she answered, "Not very well." She added that her mother was on her way from Texas to check up on her — and she was in a whole lot of trouble.

No kidding.

Deadly Habit #1:
Skip Class ... Often

It's easy to skip class. And the excuses are endless.

- I don't feel well.
- I am tired.
- I have a project due for another class.

At college, your parents aren't there to force you to go to school. Sure, some courses do have an attendance policy — such as foreign language courses and science labs. Most lecture courses do not. And some college students believe that in these cases, class attendance is optional. I hear students say that they will just get notes from a classmate and catch up. This rarely works out well for the student. And this is fairly easy to show. I simply pull up his or her last exam and, without exception, pick out which lectures the student missed by finding the cluster of items answered incorrectly. There is something important that does happen when you attend lectures.

The Game-Changer

Go to class. There are two important reasons to attend class. **First, there is no substitute for your own lecture notes.** Now you may claim that you are a horrible note-taker and that anyone's notes are surely better than yours. But I can change that for you and will get to that in Rule #3. When you attend lectures, you come to class with your own background knowledge and own organizational style. These dramatically influence the notes you will take. Think of the last time you missed class and borrowed notes from a classmate. Did you struggle to decipher them? Of course you did. Your classmates are not *you*. There is no substitute for your own lecture notes, and as you will see, these become key players in your exam preparation. I have seen borrowed lecture notes cost students a half to a full letter-grade for each missed lecture!

Second, each class period is a learning session. When you attend class, you do much more than transcribe notes. If you come prepared (see Rule #3), each lecture attended represents a valuable learning experience. You will have:
- a better understanding of the material
- better lecture notes
- better grades.

Miss a week of classes and that adds up to three hours of learning that you will never recover. Attend lectures. Learn while there. It's a game-changer.

Are there legitimate reasons why a student can miss a class? Sure. There are only three.

1) You have a deadly contagious disease that would kill off university students, faculty, and staff. Do nothing that would harm others.

> # Miss a week of classes and that adds up to three hours of learning that you will never recover.

2) You have donated a vital organ, such as a kidney, to save another person's life.

Saving another person's life through an organ donation is a wonderful thing, and I will personally re-lecture what you missed. However, you must show me the surgical scar as proof.

3) You are flat out on the delivery table giving birth to a child. Guys — you'd better be there with your wife if this is happening.

That's it. There are no other reasons for missing class. None.

Go to class. This is the easiest rule to adopt, and it is a game-changer as you begin to master course material to make better grades.

A

Rule

Never Sit
in the
Cheap Seats

Never Sit in the Cheap Seats

I like coming into class early. I first set up my multimedia slide show and then head to the back of the lecture hall to get to know those students who like to sit in the nosebleed section. Well, to be honest, I go back there to tease them. I say, "There is a perception among many faculty that all the A students sit up front. I'm curious as to whether any of you will prove that to be a myth." Most become restless in their seats and give me a smile as if to say, "don't count on me for that!"

I also like to mention that long-term university plans are to convert this part of the lecture hall into the skybox section complete with flat screen TVs on the chair backs so they can get slow motion and instant replays of awesome parts of my lectures.

"The plans also call for coolers under the seats," I tell them. The school will stock them with their favorite beverage to enjoy while the lecture plays out. Students love this idea, and maybe financially-strapped universities should be thinking about this in classroom renovation plans.

But then I add that these skybox seats would cost them a premium in tuition dollars. It would be worth it, though. For now, these seats cost just as much as those in front, which, interestingly, is completely different than any other venue — be it sports, music or otherwise. And like all of those other activities, in a lecture hall, all of the action that matters is going on in the front of the classroom.

Perhaps for now we ought to be charging more in tuition for the front-row seats.

Deadly Habit #2:
Sit in the Back Row

Students head to the back of the lecture hall for many reasons. Maybe you are a bit shy. Perhaps sitting in the back will make you feel anonymous. Or maybe you think the teacher won't call on you. This is never the case in my class. **Learning is not a spectator sport.** If you think all you have to do is just show up in order to master the material, you are wrong.

There are many things that happen while sitting in the back of class, and none of them have to do with learning. Students visit with friends. They read the online news. They eat a late breakfast or lunch. Some access the internet to watch YouTube videos, shop Amazon or peruse Facebook. In the back, some students "romance-conquest," while others even nap. This napping used to annoy me and, sometimes, I would try to correct the behavior. While tossing an eraser to wake up a student was always fun … no one uses chalkboards these days.

But I realized that all of those things really just hurt the student. And, ultimately, each student is responsible for his or her own learning. In kindergarten, we are taught that it's the teacher's job to teach and the student's job to learn.

Let's do our jobs.

The Game-Changer

Sit in the front row. And while you're at it, do not sit next to your friends. All of the good stuff you pay for happens up front. Every row you move back, you put dozens of potential distractions between you as a learner and me as a teacher. It might be someone talking about his or her date the night before. It could be a neighbor flipping through the newspaper. Maybe it is a laptop in front of you running the latest funny video posted on YouTube. Or perhaps the student seated next to you is texting about his or her plans for the evening. Trust me, those distractions do not happen in the front of the classroom.

A number of studies have shown sitting in the front of a lecture hall leads to better grades, while sitting in the back leads to more Ds and Fs. One faculty couple tracked over 1,800 students enrolled in their 70 classes during a 15-year period and found exactly that effect (Marshall and Losonczy-Marshall, 2010). I've even seen this for myself! A few years ago, on an exam in one of my 500 seat classes, I surveyed students on where they had been seated for my lectures. I found that students seated front and center in the sweet spot had an average score of 82%. Those in the middle of the lecture hall scored 72%, and those in the far back corners scored 65%. Wow-that's a two letter grade drop as you move to the back! Another study shows that getting students to move out of the back rows and up to the front pushes these terrible grades up (Benedict and Hoag, 2004). After sharing these data with my students, my classrooms now fill front to back, rather than the other way around.

And while you're at it, turn off your cell phone to avoid the distraction of text messages. Yes, even this can cost you grades, as a study by Professor Tara Lineweaver and her student Amanda Gingerich have proven [2014]. In Lineweaver's study, students in an upper division psychology class were randomly assigned into texting and no-texting groups. Texting students were given cell numbers of classmates in the same condition and asked to sustain a text conversation during a 30-minute lecture while taking notes. Despite knowing there would be a quiz afterwards, students in the texting condition scored an average of 73% while the no-text conditioned averaged 83%. That's a whole letter grade difference!

Every distraction disconnects you from the material, and you lose. Your lecture notes lose an important detail. If that detail is gone from your notes, then it is gone from your study session. This translates into missed learning and missed exam questions. If your train of thought is disrupted for just a second, it may take a minute or more for you to get back on track with the lecture. This means more missed material.

I've asked you to follow Rule #1, right? Please do not make class attendance meaningless. Make it count by following Rule #2.

Stay away from the cheap seats. Sit front and center. You'll get better grades. It's a game changer.

A

Rule #

Come to
Class Prepared

A

I like to visit with my students about how they prep for exams. I think of our conversation as a diagnostic check ... not unlike one run on your car when it is not working properly. Some say they rewrite lecture notes (a terrible idea, in my opinion). Others claim to use flashcards (but rarely in the correct manner). All talk about long study sessions the night before the exam (see Rule #5).

After listening a bit, I ask, "Well, what do you do *before* coming to my lectures?" For struggling college students, this question usually grinds their gears a bit. I can sense they are thinking: eat breakfast, brush teeth, clean up dorm room ... what the heck is Professor Sufka getting at? Some actually ask, "Am I supposed to do something before class?"

I jump in and help them out. I say, "C'mon, it's just a lecture, right? All you need to do is show up and take notes, right? Pen, paper, and some caffeinated beverage, and you're set to go, right?" Wrong. Very wrong.

Let me ask you this ... do you have difficulty in note taking and following the lectures? Do you feel overwhelmed by all of these new terms and concepts? Do you tune out? Do lectures feel like drinking water out of a fire hose? Does it feel like you can barely keep up with note taking? Does the professor's verbiage bypass the brain completely and head directly to the hand to scribble notes?

If so, you are not prepared for class. You will take unorganized and incomplete notes. And you will certainly lose points come exam time.

Come to Class Prepared

Deadly Habit #3: Come to Class Cold

I always ask my students whether they read the text assignments. Most students report that that they do (it is fairly shocking to learn that a few do not).

But my next question is what matters: "When do you read the text assignment?" More often than not, students who struggle with grades report reading the text some time *after* the lecture, or worse, a few days before the test.

It's easy to put off reading text assignments until just before the exam. Being a college student is a full-time job. Add to this full-time commitment the distraction of social engagements, extracurricular activities, perhaps a part-time job — and suddenly, classroom obligations get put on the back burner. Often, the first thing to go is required reading. This is a deadly habit. It will cost you letter grades.

The Game-Changer

Come to class prepared. I recommend three strategies to prepare for class —

Read assigned material before the lecture. At the beginning of each term, faculty post or distribute a course syllabus. A syllabus contains important information about exams, assignments, grading scales, attendance requirements, and other course policies. It also contains your course reading assignments. Owning the text but never opening it is very bad. Not reading the assignment until after a lecture is ... well, it is also very bad. You will end up with horrible lecture notes. And mastering horrible lecture notes will give you horrible grades.

Reading the text assignment before a lecture familiarizes you with key terms, concepts, and examples and creates something like a closet organizer in your mind. Women, you may have in your closet a place for your blouses, skirts, long dresses, and shoes. Guys, well, you probably just throw all of your clothes into a pile on the floor. But imagine you had a place for your jeans, sweat-shirts, dress shirts, sport coats, slacks, and so forth. The point is that a closet organizer is a place to hang stuff. Lecture content needs its own closet organizer. Read beforehand to create one for your lecture.

When first reading your text assignment, do not aim for rote memorization. Rather, read to get a general feel of the lecture content for the day.

Here's a great reading strategy. First, go to the chapter's end, review the key terms and summary statements, and then start from the beginning. Understand, your goal is to figure out what you should learn from the text before reading the chapter. This is no

"Great notes are essential to earning A grades."

different than watching the last five minutes of a whodunit movie. It is amazing the details you pick up once you know the end game. Watch *Shutter Island* a second time and you will know exactly what I mean. Reading before a lecture creates a sort of road map ... or closet organizer.

Students who do this follow my lectures much better, understand difficult concepts, and end up with very thorough and well-organized lecture notes. And great notes are essential to earning A grades. But something more important happens when you do these things. You transform yourself from just a note-taker during lectures to being a learner and a note-taker.

Come to lecture when you're sharpest. Come to class cognitively alert. You must get a good night's sleep. Get some caffeine in your system. For those afternoon classes, take a short nap before class. I once came across a study that showed students who took a ten-minute nap before an exam earned better scores. I would bet a short nap before class would result in better lecture notes and more classroom learning.

Remember, you have to bring your A game to the lecture hall each and every time. So come to class when you're at your best.

And while you're at it, put your laptop back into your backpack and pull out a paper tablet for note-taking. Yes, even laptop note-taking can cost you grades, as a study by Professors Pam Mueller and Daniel Oppenheimer (2014) have shown. In their experiments, students were randomly assigned into laptop or longhand note-taking groups, then watched a TED Talk and afterwards, took a quiz. In each and every experiment, laptop note-takers were able to produce more overall words in their notes than longhand note-takers. This should not surprise anyone, as many students prefer laptops for note-taking because of the ease at transcribing lecture material. The problem shows up on quiz performance. Long-hand note-takers significantly outscored laptop note-takers by 0.3 to 0.4 z-scores on conceptual level questions (I'll say more about these in Chapter 7). As I tell my students, simply transcribing a lecture verbatim bypasses all the good stuff in your brain necessary for learning and memory. Reframing lecture content into your own words routes such information through brain networks for comprehension leading to better material mastery and increased grades. Findings from studies like Mueller and Oppenheimer's suggest I should simply ban laptops in the classroom; it would be for your own good!

Record lectures. If you are a slow note taker, ask permission to record the lectures. My experience is that most faculty are open to recording devices in the classroom.

If you record, you can replay the lectures to fill in missing parts. Students tell me they re-listen to my lectures while driving home for a weekend visit to their parents. It's another learning opportunity — and another game changer.

I think of mastering course material as a cascade of strategic elements that must occur in the correct order. Good lecture preparation leads to better organized, more thorough notes. Better notes for exam preparation means better learning and retention. And better retention translates into better exam grades. Further, coming to class prepared will transform the lecture experience from simply note taking, like a court reporter, to having an actual learning experience while taking notes. Learning while in the classroom puts you further ahead in mastering course content.

Rule

When Lost,
Ask Questions

A

My colleague Professor Kelly Wilson has an office directly across from mine in the psychology department. Sporting shoulder-length hair, trendy eyeglasses, and Prada loafers, Professor Wilson practices yoga six days a week. In the classroom — and office — his teaching is a no-holds-barred, in-your-face, smack-down kind of experience. I should also mention he is an award-winning teacher and inspiring psychotherapy workshop leader. He is also one damn funny man.

Several years ago I overheard him talking with one of his students. Professor Wilson seemed frustrated by the student, but I could not imagine what led him to ask the following question: "Do you want to feel stupid? Or do you want to be stupid?"

This seemed a little confrontational to me. So after the student left, I walked into Professor Wilson's office.

"What was that all about?" I asked.

It seems this young woman was getting lost in class, but she was unwilling to raise her hand to ask for clarifications.

"She was afraid she would look dumb in front of her classmates," Professor Wilson said.

So she sat in class, completely lost in the course material — and then tuned out during the rest of the lecture.

Professor Wilson's query makes an excellent point. You can choose to look stupid to your classmates in order to avoid being stupid. Or, you can choose to stay stupid and avoid the embarrassment of looking stupid. The smart (non-stupid) option is pretty clear to me: raise your hand when you have a question.

When Lost, Ask Questions

The A Game

Deadly Habit #4:
Aim for Anonymity

Aim for classroom anonymity. How might you accomplish this:

- Avoid embarrassing situations.
- Sit in the back of the classroom (violates Rule #2).
- Remain quiet when you are completely lost.
- Leave the classroom dazed and confused.
- Never ever approach your professor with any questions. I call those who practice these deadly habits "Stealth Students."

I never hear from them. And in some situations, I never see them (remember Rule #1) until it is exam time. I swear I have given exams in large classes and have noticed "new" faces. Worse is the *stealth student* who has attended most of the lectures, failed all of the exams, and then comes to see me days before the final exam to ask if I know of anything that will help him or her pass. This is when I want to hand over a set of rosary beads, recommend saying several dozen *Hail Marys*, a few *Our Fathers*, and suggest they pray for divine intervention.

At this point, it is impossible for me to help them pass. It is simply too late.

The Game-Changer

This game changer is easy. **Raise your hand when you have a question.** If a concept or idea needs clarification, it is critical that you ask in order to follow the rest of the lecture.

You know when this is happening. Your note taking style will shift to that of a court reporter (in the ear and out the hand).

When professors have lectured for many years, they tend to know where problem areas arise and can recognize certain facial expressions (like the one where students look completely baffled). But the truth is that none of us are mind readers. Remember, our job is to teach and your job is to learn. If you're lost, you're not learning. And I need you to stay on the learning job, so ask questions. Please.

Excellent lecture notes are vital to master course content and get excellent grades. Further, you have to remember: each lecture can be a learning experience. It's more than a transcript-taking enterprise. If you **hit a snag, get it clarified** so the rest of the lecture continues to make sense.

Take advantage of a professor's office hours. Be a sponge. Soak up knowledge.

Professor Wilson told me when he was a student he spent so much time in one of his professor's office that he had his own coffee cup. Wilson added, "College is like an all-you-can-eat buffet. Why are students so finicky about filling up their plate? It's deeply mysterious to me." So remember, fill up your plates. Get intellectually engaged with the course material. Make a connection with your teacher. And keeping going back for more.

> "If you are lost, you are not learning. So ask questions, please."

Office Hours Etiquette

Here are my suggestions for stopping by to visit professors during office hours. No faculty will respond favorably to a student coming to office hours expecting a re-lecture, regardless of the reason (except, of course, in the event of a kidney donation). A re-lecture is impractical. **We all have busy schedules.** We teach dozens, if not hundreds of students. Of the more than 300 students I teach each semester, somewhere between 30 and 50 (or more!) will miss a lecture during the week. There is no way I could re-lecture that many times. But that does not mean faculty are unwilling to help clarify lecture material.

Do not expect the lecture to be completely mastered once you leave the classroom. That's not realistic. You will need to go back through your notes and back to the textbook for additional clarification. Later, I will show you how to begin mastering course content. Do keep track of areas in the lecture that you don't understand. Your professor will need that list for your office visit. For the time being, don't panic. Understand that few people learn without great effort. For most of us, it is going to be hard work.

When you come by for an office visit, please be prepared to tell me, specifically, the content that needs clarification. You might even prepare this in the form of a list of questions. A good starting point: tell me what you do know. This tells me that you have some mastery of the lecture material. I also like my students to attempt to describe the material they think they *do not* know. This gives me the best starting point to help you master course content. Now, I only have a portion of the lecture to review, and it is much easier to facilitate your understanding. Preparation for an office visit enables us both to be highly effective and efficient.

If you follow these guidelines, I do not mind how often you come by my office. Neither will most faculty. As a motivated learner, you will always be welcomed. You might even earn a spot for your very own coffee cup.

Rule

Get Spaced Out

A

A couple of semesters ago, Steven, a general psychology student, stopped by my office. He had not done well on the first test and was hoping to get some tips on how to better prepare. Steven had attended all of the lectures. He tended to sit toward the front, away from friends and distractions. Most of the time, he kept up with the reading assignments. So, I decided to look over his exam to glean some insight. Perhaps he was missing certain kinds of questions. Maybe he was getting the factual information correct but was not able to apply this knowledge.

In the process of hand-grading his exam, I discovered a clear pattern of correct and incorrect responses. I knew immediately the poor grades could be caused by only one thing.

I looked at Steven and boldly asserted, "You pulled an all-nighter."

By the expression on his face I could tell he was dumbfounded. How could I possibly know that Steven had, in fact, stayed up all night studying for the exam? Did I see this on his Facebook page?

What I saw was something cognitive psychologists call the "serial position effect." It is most often seen when someone tries to learn a long list of items in a short period of time.

To illustrate the serial position effect, I will ask you to perform an exercise. And then I'll show you how to avoid falling into this trap that leads to miserable exam performance.

Get Spaced Out

Deadly Habit #5: Pull All-Nighters

It's easy to put off studying until the last minute. Most students think that it is simply a matter of the *amount* of time you put into studying that counts. Sure, time does matter. No reasonable person would argue that one hour of study time equates to eight hours of study time. But what really matters is the amount of *quality* study time. In the course of an eight-hour, all-night study session, the amount of quality time you actually put in is probably no more than a couple of hours. The rest is a complete waste of time. And it can actually work against you.

Serial Position Effect Exercise

Let's conduct a little experiment (**see Exercise 1, page 32**). It is a simple memory experiment. I need you to slowly read through a list of letters and then recall that list. Now you will need a card or a sheet of paper to cover the letters. Read the list of letters once in the order presented, about one item per second. Then, cover up the list with your index card and immediately try to recall that list — but do so in the same order they were presented. I'll even give you a hint by listing the number of letters to be filled in. See how many you get correct. Don't forget the index card.

Results

Let's take a look at the number you got correct from each list. I am guessing you got 100% on the first list and 90-95% or better on the second list. That third list was a little tougher. Now look at what happened on the fourth and fifth lists. Not so good? It is not uncommon to get 40-50% recall accuracy. Now I want you to look at the fourth and fifth lists a little more closely. Did you notice that you tended to get the first several items correct on the list and then maybe the last one or two items? You have just experienced the limits of your cognition and produced your very own serial position curve.

Exercise #1

Read list (about one letter per second).
Cover with index card and recall in order presented.

List #1

— — — —

c y h g

List #2

— — — — — — —

x n q f c r j m

List #3

— — — — — — — — — —

k h p i x z q f s v j t

List #4

— — — — — — — — — — — — —

e v t g w h d t b q a o t y k j

List #5

— — — — — — — — — — — — — — —

k l q t j m b d a z n c v e y h s y r w

The A Game

The typical serial position curve looks like the one depicted in **Figure 1** and plots the percent recall as a function of the location of the item in the list. On long memory lists, you can see that a person's recall of items at the beginning is very high. This is called the *primacy effect*. Learning a small amount of new information when you are fresh is easy. Notice that the recall of items in the middle of the list is horrible. The problem is that you have exceeded the capacity of your working memory. Now there are a few items at the end of the list that tend to be recalled better than those from the middle. This is called the *recency effect*.

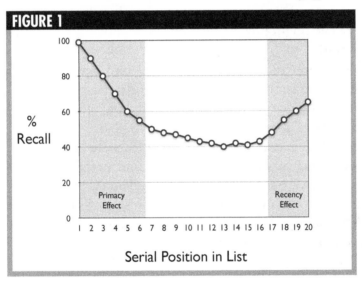

FIGURE 1

% Recall

Primacy Effect

Recency Effect

Serial Position in List

When you try to learn all of the material in one sitting, you are creating the conditions to produce the serial position curve. When I looked over Steven's exam, he tended to get many questions correct from the beginning of the test, answered few beyond chance level correctly during a large portion of the middle of the exam and then managed to get a few more correct at the very end. This is the classic pattern of an all-night study session. I see it all the time and even in very good students. Just a few semesters ago, a student in my brain and behavior class turned in an exam but didn't want to get instant feedback. This was unusual since he had done so well on earlier exams. I looked and he had scored 90% on material from the first and second lectures but then 40-

50% on the remaining three lectures. His excuse was he had three exams that week and didn't start studying on this one until it was too late. What could have been an A went to an F.

Here is what's most irritating — during the middle and end of an all-night study session, you are rarely studying much beyond a 40% or 50% level of course mastery. On my grading scale, that turns out to be an F. **Why would you spend any time studying to get an F?** That's insane! Moreover, when you add those last six hours of study time on the session, it causes increased interference with the material you learned at the beginning of the study session. What was probably learned well, say better than 95% recall, might now be recalled at only 80%. That cost you a letter grade.

Never ever undo good learning — and never try to learn when you are least able. What a waste of time.

Some students seem to treat the all-night study session as a kind of rite-of-passage and wear it as a badge of honor. What is remarkable is that many students never learn that all-nighters are the least effective way to study. They blame their failure on other factors, believing that length of time studying is the predictor of grades. This and other forms of cramming are deadly habits that are inefficient and ineffective in course material mastery. It will cost you big-time letter grades.

The Game-Changer

Space out your study sessions. If you are accustomed to an eight-hour all-nighter, next time try four days of two-hour study sessions each (Rules #6-8 will show what you need to do during those sessions). Better yet, try eight daily one-hour sessions. Better yet, try ten 90-minute sessions (ok, so I'm not a math professor).

One more piece of advice comes from Professsors John Donovan and David Radosevich (1999) who conducted a meta-analyses of 63 studies comparing spaced out study sessions against those massed together. Not surprisingly, students with opportunities to spread out study sessions easily outperformed those students who did not. But what researchers also found was that when being tested over rigorous and challenging lecture and text material, like that seen in upper division classes, the best performances came from students who not only spread out study session, but who also took a day off in between. This means that in these kinds of classes, you really need to start studying for exams two to three weeks in advance.

One other problem is that today's students study far less than the generation or two before. I recently read a paper published in 1935 that sampled students at four major universities and showed that students studied about 4.5 hours per day during the week and a bit less during the weekend (Williamson, 1935). That's nearly 30 hours per week outside of classroom time 75 years ago! A recent survey at the University of California system found students spend closer to 13 hours per week studying. What are students doing with all this extra time? Well, according to the survey, students spend more than 11 hours per week on social media and gaming. No wonder so many students struggle with course material mastery.

If you break up the amount of course material into smaller and smaller chunks and then devote small, focused study sessions to them, you will have much better recall and much better grades. For example, on the memory recall lists, you probably answered lists 1 and 2 with near perfect recall. Why? You never exceeded your cognitive limits. The most effective and efficient study sessions should be targeted toward material mastery in the range of 90% to 100%. Most cognitive psychologists think that studying much beyond two hours begins to work against good learning.

Getting spaced out with your study sessions takes some serious time-management skills. You have to be disciplined enough to commit to studying a little bit every day. Yes, every day. You are probably taking five or six classes each term, and all of them need your attention. So you need to break up your nightly study sessions with catching up with friends, watching your favorite TV show, enjoying dinner (is that possible on campus?), Facebook time and/or workouts at the gym. But you had better be hitting two or three subjects per day. Now do not worry about committing three or more hours per day to studying as long as you switch subjects. Your history course will not interfere with your psychology course, which will not interfere with your mathematics course.

One more thing about your study sessions: You not only need to keep them short, focused and spaced out, you must also be mindful of scheduling them when you are at your cognitive best.

• When are you sleepy?
• When are you alert?

For example, I never schedule anything important right after lunchtime when I am apt to slip into a food coma. On the other hand, I try to do all of my writing, like writing this book, during the morning hours after a good night's rest and several strong cups of coffee.

Know when you are at your best. Then plan your study sessions accordingly. It's a vital step in your A game. And a key to becoming a strategic learner.

A

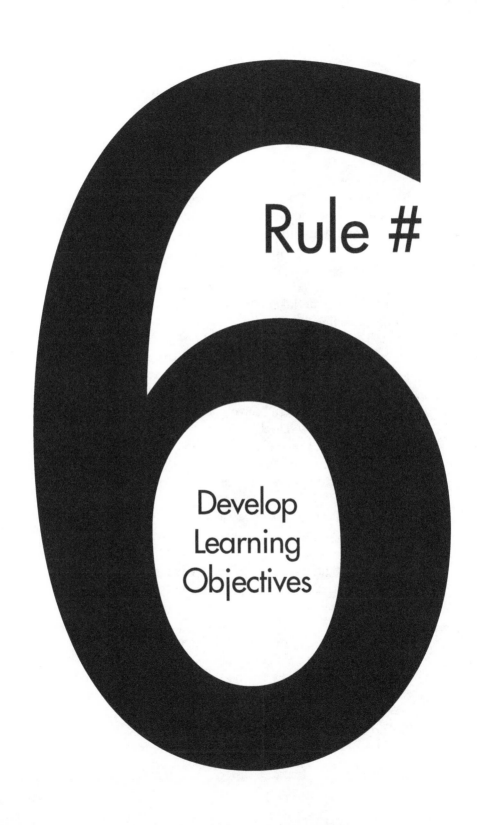

Rule #

6

Develop
Learning
Objectives

My friends' son Jimmy, who was new to college, stopped by my office to get tips on studying. He sat down and made himself at home.

"Jimmy," I asked, "what do you do during study sessions?"

"I look over my notes," he said.

"Do you go through them a second and third time?" I asked. He told me he did. "That's excellent," I said. "Repetition is important. Jimmy," I asked, "do you ever get a chance to look them over a fourth or fifth time?"

"No, not really," he answered. "Maybe if time permits."

"So," I asked, "how do you know when you have learned the material and can go on?" I paused and said, "Is it a 'gut feeling'?"

"Yeah, something like that," he responded.

This conversation was the foundation upon which I would illustrate how Jimmy's approach was ineffective in preparing for exams.

"Jimmy," I asked, "have you ever seen a penny?" He gave me a confused look.

"A penny," I repeated, "from the U.S. mint."

"Yes, of course."

"How many times?" I asked. "A hundred times? Maybe a thousand?"

"Yes," he said, "probably lots more."

"So ... you know what a penny looks like?"

"Sure," he said.

How about you? Do you know what a penny looks like? Take a look at Exercise 2 (see page 40) and tell me which one is the real penny.

Remember, you have looked at pennies more than a thousand times, many more times than you will ever look at your notes. Can't pick out the real penny, can you? Why? Well, you never really learned what a penny looks like. It has crossed through your hand countless times, not unlike your lecture notes crossing in front of you during a study session.

Jimmy picked H — good guess, but H is incorrect.

Deadly Habit #6:
Study Like a Zombie

Most students who perform poorly on exams approach study sessions with horribly ineffective and inefficient study techniques. They go through their lecture notes and re-read them. Many students also re-read the highlighted parts of the textbook. Some even re-write their lecture notes. All horrible techniques.

Many students think, after failing the first exam, that they have just not spent enough time with their notes, and they then commit more of the same ineffective study strategies. They get the same outcome on the next exam. Albert Einstein once said *insanity* is doing the same thing over and over again and expecting different results. To use the same ineffective study techniques cannot and will not improve your performance.

When you simply look over your notes, you process information at a superficial level — just like the penny passing across your palm.

This ineffective strategy will cause the following experience: You read the question. Look over the choices. You might be able to eliminate one or two of the alternatives or foils (that's what test-writers call them). But the remaining two or three all look like they could be correct. Be honest. You've had that experience. It is just like the penny trick. I bet you could narrow down the penny choices to a few alternatives, but beyond that you were just flat out guessing. How do you keep from falling for the penny trick — where all the answers look correct? That is easy. I want you to take a different approach to studying.

The Game-Changer

For each study session, you must have clear and concise learning objectives. State exactly what you want to learn. This must be very clear.

Exercise #2

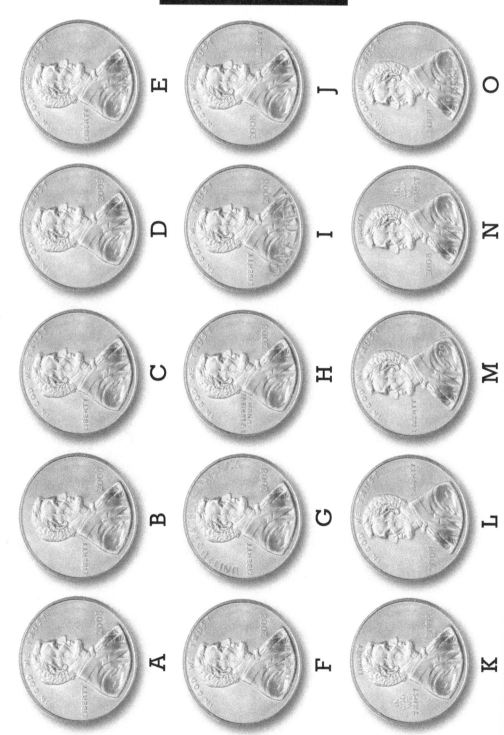

Which one is the real penny?
For full-color illustration, visit www.TheAGameBook.com

If you have excellent notes, this is easy. Allow me to illustrate how to develop learning objectives. Let's return to the penny. Go find one.

I am going to assume that you knew President Lincoln is depicted on the penny, but there are a few more details to learn.

First, which way is Lincoln facing? He is facing to your right.

Second, where is the date located? The date is located in the lower right.

Third, where is the word *Liberty* located? *Liberty* is located on the left side of the coin.

Fourth, where is the phrase *In God We Trust* located? That phrase is found across the top of the coin.

So there you have your four learning objectives. If you want to be able to correctly identify a penny, you just need to know those four things. Four simple learning objectives: 1) Lincoln faces to your right; 2) Date located on the right; 3) *Liberty* located on the left; and 4) *In God We Trust* located across top.

Now to make them fun and memorable, let's elaborate on them a bit. How can we re-work *Lincoln faces to your right*? He is considered one of the greatest Presidents. How about *Lincoln was always right*?

What's up next? *Date* located on the right. Oh, I got one. Think boyfriend or girlfriend. You never ever turn your back on your date — always face your date. Lincoln was always right, and he faced his date. Does that work? Face your date!

Next up is *Liberty* on the left. Hmmm. Liberty-left. Liberty-left. Liberty-left. Dang, can't think of anything. How about you? Oh, L-L. Liberty-left. So now we have *Lincoln was always right, face your date, and liberty-left*.

Last one is *In God We Trust* located across the top. So you're telling me God is up there on top or on high, right? That works for me. God on high.

There we have it. Four learning objectives: 1) Lincoln was always right; 2) face your date; 3) Liberty-left; and 4) God on high. Let's say them again. Lincoln was always right, face your date, Liberty-left and God on high. Close your eyes and repeat them again. Got them down? Bet you do.

If you come to class well prepared (see Rule #3) and obtain excellent lecture notes, identifying learning objectives is easy. In some cases, it is information from a table or diagram. Some faculty use extensive outlines, and that can be very helpful. Each helps you to develop learning objectives. By the way, what were the four learning objectives of the

"Learning objectives are useful in any class."

penny? Bet you recalled them. See how easy that was?

Learning objectives are useful in any class. Consider a history course and some event in the past. Identify the event, who the players were, what the causes of that event were, and what the consequences of that event were. For each of these you will likely have sub-level learning objectives. For example, the learning objectives for the consequences might be considered in economical, military, political, and social terms, among others. This talk of developing learning objectives with main headings and sub-headings is very similar to a great study technique called concept mapping.

Concept Mapping

Concept mapping is a strategy people use to organize and make sense of knowledge much like road maps are created to organize highways, towns, parks, rivers, lakes, and so forth. Think of this "knowledge organizer" much in the same way you have a closet organizer for your clothes, shoes, and wardrobe accessories. Yes, that's the same closet organizer I mentioned back in Chapter 3. More importantly, concept maps promote more meaningful learning and better retention because you connect key concepts and ideas in an organized manner (Nesbitt and Adesope, 2006).

Concept maps were originally developed by Cornell Professor Joseph D. Novak to, not surprisingly, enhance student learning — particularly in the more challenging disciplines like the physical sciences. How concept maps work is reasonably straightforward. It is based on the notion that new knowledge is created when linked to existing knowledge. In psychology, this kind of learning is called assimilation. For those of you who are *Star Trek: The Next Generation* fans, this is the same kind of knowledge acquisition of The Borg.

Constructing a concept map is a straight-forward process, especially if you have well-organized lecture notes (see Rule #3). For any concept map, you begin with a particular domain of knowledge and then fit in the pieces of information to show how they connect to one another. You have seen these before if you have ever watched a crime drama. Here detectives try to link together the criminal players and their motives.

"Concept maps promote more meaningful learning and better retention."

Imagine a lecture covering the concept of seasons. The professor presents information that includes definitions, concepts, and examples. The goal of concept mapping is to organize this information in a manner that will ultimately facilitate learning and retention. In this lecture you learn —the names of seasons, the temperatures and length of sunlight associated with each season, how the tilting orbit of the earth causes seasonal variations. How one might assemble all of these lecture elements into a concept map is given in Figure 2 (**on page 44**).

In this concept map you see major ideas listed in boxes. More importantly, you see arrows between boxes, which detail the connections between the concepts. Some of the connections between boxes highlight simple features (e.g., length of day longer in summer) while others highlight deeper connections (e.g., height of sun above horizon is determined by the degree of tilt of the earth's axis).

In my lectures, I organize material to make concept maps easy to construct. I provide students a basic lecture outline. From this, students fill in the details. For example, a concept map of my out-

FIGURE 2

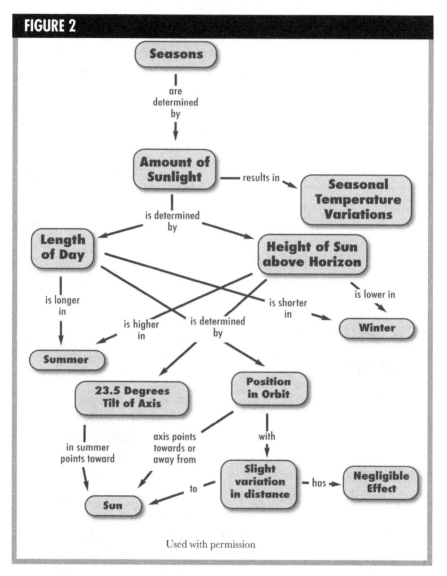

Used with permission

line of schizophrenia in my biopsychology class would entail organizing knowledge around 1) symptoms, 2) causes, 3) neuropathology, and 4) treatment. Each of these four boxes (or nodes) would have sub-nodes of their own. For example, symptoms of schizophrenia cluster about two broad categories. Higher levels of learning appear through links. If you attended my lecture, you would easily find crosslinks among these major cate- gories. The node of one category of symptoms can be linked to a sub-node under pathology (excess dopamine), which can be linked to a sub-node under treatment (with thorazine).

Connecting concepts together represents the deepest understanding of material.

A recent study by Professors Jack Berry and Stephen Chew (2008) shows that simply making concept maps increases test performance. In their experiment, Berry and Chew gave general psychology students extra credit for creating up to two concept maps for an upcoming quiz. Each concept map, which had been discussed earlier in the term, had to have at least 30 interlinked concepts or nodes.

Some students submitted maps with many more nodes, and one map had 95 nodes.

Students who submitted concept maps had better exam scores than students who did not. Further, students who submitted two maps had better exam scores than those who submitted only one. Finally, students who submitted maps with more nodes had better exam scores than students submitting maps with fewer nodes. Just making concept maps facilitated

> **"Making concept maps during study sessions increases test performance."**

learning. In Chapter 8, I will show you another rule to follow using these concept maps for better learning outcomes. In other words, better grades.

Four-Question Reflective Learning

Another approach to develop learning objectives from your lecture material comes from psychology Professors Beth Dietz-Uhler and Jason Lanter (2009). They had students use a four-question reflective learning exercise prior to taking a quiz. The exercise is designed to encourage **active learning** on the part of the student. Active learning has been shown to promote better retention of material and enhance test performance.

Students were asked to provide 100-word written responses to each of four questions. The four questions were 1) identify an important concept, research finding, theory, or idea in psychology; 2) explain why this concept, finding, theory, or idea is important; 3) explain how this concept, finding, theory, or idea applies to some aspect of your life; and 4) identify what questions are left unanswered for you regarding this concept, finding, theory, or idea. The first three questions are essentially learning objectives: identify a concept, explain why it is important, and detail how it applies to your life. As you will see in the next chapter, these kinds of questions tap into higher levels of learning, too. Students who performed the learning exercise during study time had 15% higher scores than those who did not — even with the same amount of study time. That is a letter grade and a half increase in scores!

"A four-question reflective learning exercise can increase your scores by 15%."

Notation Reduction

One of my professors taught me this learning strategy, and my students love this technique because it works so darned well. If you choose this strategy, you must begin at least a week or two before the exam. The technique is called notation reduction.

The objective is to gather all of your lecture notes and compile them in a version that fits on a single notebook page. Think of this as a big cheat sheet. Notation reduction requires some serious processing of information. You are reducing a large amount of material into key phrases, concepts, and examples. The idea is that you should be able to recall everything on the original set of notes by your cues on the cheat-sheet. This should be completed about one week out from the exam. At this point, I review the sheet for gaping holes. I trust your professor will do the same.

Now, once you have accomplished that learning objective (remember to save some space for subsequent lectures), I want you to take that full cheat-sheet page and reduce it to a 5" x 8" card. Yes, that will take some work. But if you can reduce those notes to this level, you'll process information even deeper. Now your learning objective is to be able to look at that card and answer any question in your original set of notes. You should complete the small cheat-sheet at least three to four days out from the exam. Again, I review your 5" x 8" cheat-card. I also throw a few questions at you to check your learning. But we're not quite finished.

"Students love notation reduction because it works so darn well."

Finally, you need a 3" x 5" note card. Your task is to reduce your 5" x 8" cheat-sheet to this 3" x 5" card. This sounds difficult — all of your lecture notes on a 3" x 5" cheat-card. But it is actually pretty easy to do at this point. In addition to this notation reduction step, I have one more objective.

One day before the exam, I want you to be able to take that 3" x 5" card, turn it over and recreate the entire content from memory. Actually, most students eventually do this with no problem. Once you re-create the notes from memory, you will have created a cheat-card in your mind's eye. From that 3" x 5" mental card, you have all the cues necessary to recall vast amounts of information.

Come exam time, if you need to, data dump. As soon as you are handed the test booklet, recreate your cheat-card on the back. This is not cheating. It is knowing and understanding the course material. Completely.

One of the biggest game changers is the ability to develop learning objectives. It sets out a clear path in getting A grades on your exams. A friend of mine from Furman University, Professor Charles Brewer, says, "If you don't know where you are going, the chance of getting there approaches randomness."

In exam preparation and exam taking, randomness is failing. Trust me, I have seen exam scores that are below chance-level performance. Maybe I should add another grade category to my courses: an LF grade for Legendary Failure.

Developing learning objectives is absolutely necessary to bring your A game to the classroom. It gives you a clear path to follow in your studying and avoids the outcome of random responses come exam time. But there is more to discover about those learning objectives. Let's move to Rule #7.

A

Rule #7

Learn Material at All Levels

A

Several years ago, a student from my general psychology class came to my office to look over his exam. He said he was shocked to learn that he had failed. "Who isn't?" I said.

"But I walked in feeling like I knew the material," he said.

The young man had attended every lecture (Rule #1) and had always taken a seat up close and away from friends (Rule #2). He admitted to rarely looking at the text assignments before class (violation of Rule #3). He was a bit quiet in class (violation of Rule #4), but I had to give him credit for coming up to see me so early in the term to get on the right track. For exam preparation, he said he studied two or three days before the test (could probably do better with Rule #5), as all-nighters never worked for him. In asking how he approached studying, he said he relied mostly on flash cards (which is one way to make learning objectives Rule #6) and that he had indeed been able to answer all of them correctly (see upcoming Rule #8). I was baffled. How could this young man make these claims and not score better than 50% on the test material?

"May I take a look at your flash cards?" I asked.

"Sure," he said, pulling them from his backpack. "Quiz me on any of them."

I started looking through the rather large pile of flash cards. Sure enough, key terms were given on one side and the correct definition provided on the reverse. After carefully examining the first half dozen or so I quickly thumbed through the remainder of the cards. I spotted the problem immediately. Out of curiosity, I did ask him to recall a few flash cards, and, sure enough, he nailed the answers. I then went to his exam, hand-scored it, and confirmed the problem. So what was it? It was the *Dragnet* effect.

Back in the 1950s and 60s there was a police show on television called *Dragnet*. The main character was Detective Joe Friday, who was interested in gathering "just the facts." And this is exactly what got this student into trouble. He mastered 100% of the facts, but scored 0% on all of the other kinds of knowledge tested on that exam. He just didn't study at all levels of learning.

Deadly Habit #7: Study Just the Facts

Students often find themselves with a limited amount of study time. Some head for the glossary of key terms and study only that material. Perhaps they have never been tested at higher levels of learning. This may have worked reasonably well for them in the past. But nearly all college teachers expect a great deal more from their students and test them accordingly. Certainly, learning the facts is a necessary foundation to greater understanding. But learning just the facts is a far cry from mastering course material. Avoid the **Dragnet effect**. Learning *only* the items in bold or the glossary is a deadly habit.

The Game Changer

Learning occurs in a hierarchy. Mastering lower-level information enables higher levels of learning and understanding. These higher levels of learning move beyond just knowing something. It is a bit like the difference between knowing *that something happened* and knowing *how* and *why it happened*. Indeed, students who can apply basic facts and concepts understand material at a higher level. And trust me when I say this: I will test you at these higher levels of learning, as will most faculty.

One of the most frequently used models to characterize this notion is *Bloom's Taxonomy of Learning* (Bloom, 1956). The taxonomy is typically depicted as a six-level, pyramid-shaped model that is hierarchically organized. Information at the lowest level must be mastered in order to step up to the next level of learning. Bloom's levels of learning are shown on the left side of the pyramid in Figure 3 (**see Figure 3, page 52**).

To explain this concept to my students, I cluster Bloom's six categories around three levels of knowledge. Those categories appear to the right of the pyramid. I consider factual knowledge to be at the lowest level of learning. It includes Bloom's categories knowledge and comprehension. At this level, you master key terms

FIGURE 3

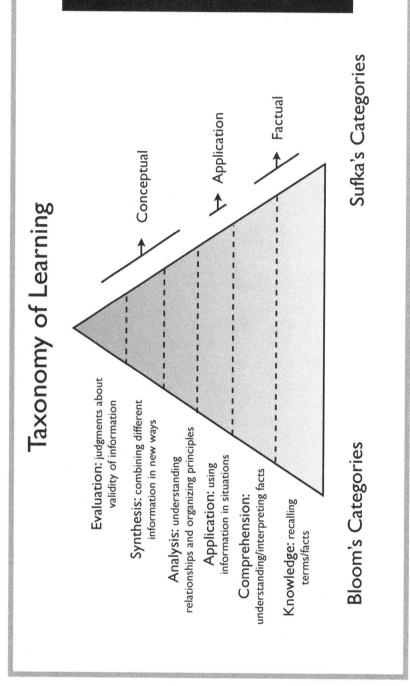

Taxonomy of Learning

Sufka's Categories

Conceptual

Application

Factual

Bloom's Categories

Evaluation: judgments about validity of information

Synthesis: combining different information in new ways

Analysis: understanding relationships and organizing principles

Application: using information in situations

Comprehension: understanding/interpreting facts

Knowledge: recalling terms/facts

and concepts. This is the kind of learning that relies on mastering definitions and organizing your knowledge into concept maps. A test question based on factual knowledge might be, "Which of the following is the best definition of classical conditioning?" This level of learning is the foundation upon which higher learning is built. But do not stop here!

The next level of learning in my model is application knowledge (the same as Bloom's). Students take factual knowledge and apply it to real-world situations. A test question based on application knowledge might require a student to identify a concept found in a narrative. For example, "What conditioning principle describes the phenomenon of a person's becoming sad when seeing a dog that resembles a beloved family pet from his or her childhood?"

Here, I expect you to recognize a real-world application of a common learning principle. People who can use knowledge in a variety of applied settings have achieved a higher level of learning and, on tests, earn higher grades.

Finally, at the top of my learning hierarchy is conceptual knowledge. At this level, a student can take sets of facts and examples from related — or seemingly disparate — topics, compare and contrast them, and use them in novel ways. This is the highest level of learning. A conceptual knowledge test question from my biopsychology exam might be, "Why do antipsychotic medications, like thorazine, produce Parkinson-like symptoms?" Here a student would need to know and link together the mechanisms of the action of thorazine and the neuropathology of Parkinson's disease. This would indicate the deepest understanding of course material. And at test time, this earns A grades.

> "Multi-level learning objectives are essential to achieve excellent grades."

In concept mapping, ensure you add sub-nodes of application knowledge. To tap into conceptual-level learning, look for links between nodes. Ask questions about how they connect — or do not. You must fit multi-level learning objectives into your game plan to achieve A grades. Why do you need to know this? Most college-level tests will contain questions at all three levels. When I create a test, about 50% of my questions tap into factual knowledge, 35% into application knowledge and 15% into conceptual knowledge. Tracy, a student from from my biopsychology class, took the same flashcard study approach and experienced the *Dragnet* effect. She scored thirty-nine out of fifty-five possible points on Exam 1. Looking more closely at the missed questions, I showed her she only missed one factual question. That's nearly 100% mastery… of the lowest level of learning. Of the other fifteen she missed, eleven were application and four conceptual-type questions.

Do you now understand how the *Dragnet* effect leads to failing grades? On half of the test, you'll get most of the questions correct. On the remaining half, you will perform around chance-level. That should translate into a D or F. But if you ensure that your objectives (see Rule #6) address all levels of learning, you will master course material across the entire hierarchy. This is a game changer. And you will earn A grades.

A

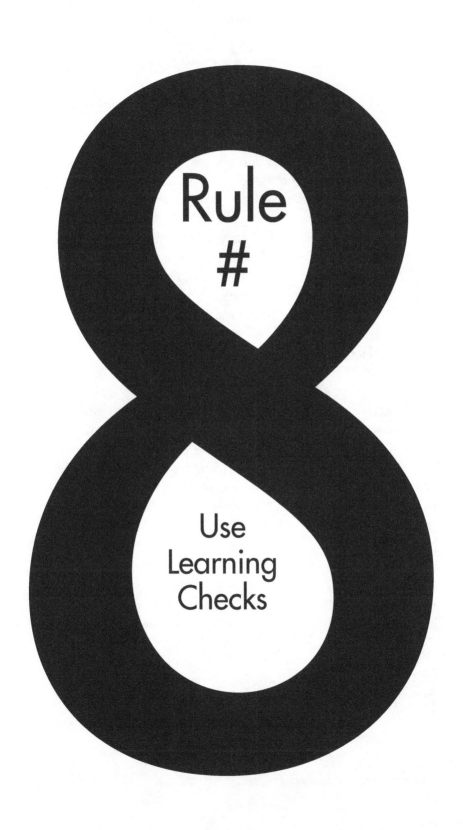

Rule
#

Use
Learning
Checks

A

Here's another story from the office of Professor Kelly Wilson. "But Dr. Wilson," a female student said to my colleague across the hall, "I made flashcards."

"Divide the cards into two piles," Professor Wilson instructed. He told the student to put all the cards she had mastered into one pile; the second was for cards she had not mastered.

To be efficient with valuable study time, Professor Wilson argued, she needed to study the flashcards she got wrong. And when she got them all correct, she should shuffle the cards and repeat the process with all the cards.

This exchange made me think about studying and learning in a broader sense.

How do we know what we know?

How do we know what we do not know?

As I noted in an earlier chapter, students often assess their knowledge by going with that "gut feeling" after running through their notes several times. And we know how that doesn't work. Remember the penny trick?

A few weeks later, a student came in during office hours. He had not done well on the first two exams. He was getting about 50% of the material correct. He had violated most of my rules and was sitting solidly on an F grade.

Trying to cheer him up, I said, "Do you realize that on half of the test items you scored 100%? That's a perfect score and an A grade." A big smile came to his face. And although I knew this was going to take the wind out of his sail, I added, "It is the other half of the test that you missed every stinking question. Zero percent correct." But I added, "I know an easy solution to figuring out what you know ... and what you don't know."

If you adopt this strategy, it will turn you into an amazingly efficient learning machine.

Use Learning Checks

Deadly Habit #8: Not Knowing That You Don't Know Jack

Never ever determine what you know and what you do not know. For some students this is apparently a mystery to be revealed by the test itself. But Professor Wilson argues that for every test you ever take, you *should* already know your score. There should be no surprises.

Another deadly habit is simply reading over and over the material until it is time to take the test. We already know this is a horrible learning strategy (see Rule #6). When you do this, you treat all the material equally. You assume you are learning it all at the same rate and depth. But that is clearly not the case. Take my student. We know that he learned half of the material really well. It's the other half that he needed to really study. Think about this. You test yourself, and you get an item correct. You can't score higher than that, right? So stop wasting your time on the stuff you already know. It costs you valuable study time. It also costs you grades.

The Game-Changer

Use learning checks in your study sessions. And do so often. It is important to segregate information that is well-learned from that which is not. Just like when Dr. Wilson asked his student to sort her flash cards into two piles. Study time is valuable. You should not waste it on learning material you already know. Your study time should always be devoted to learning new information and to self-testing to confirm that you retain it.

There is another important thing that happens when you check your learning through self-tests. Studies show that retrieval practice on self-tests improves scores more than other study techniques like concept mapping. There are three key strategies to check your learning during study sessions. They are game changers in mastering course content and in getting A grades.

White-Board Learning Checks

Start with a white board and some dry erase markers. Your goal is to re-create a learning objective without referring to notes. For example, I want students to know some things about the four paradigms of operant conditioning. These are procedures that alter behavior by either giving or withholding rewarding (money) or aversive (time out periods) stimuli. A student should be able to a) name all four paradigms, b) explain the use of stimuli, c) state the effects on behavior, and d) give an example of that paradigm. We have clear learning objectives (Rule #6) coupled with higher levels of learning (Rule #7).

In my lecture, I have a highly visual scheme (a 2" x 2" four-box grid) for covering these details. Perhaps you will choose to adopt the learning strategy of creating concept maps. Either of these will work.

OK, close your notes, take out the dry erase board, and recreate the grid or concept map. Check against your notes. Did you get it all correct? If so, then move on. If not, what parts did you miss? Focus on making the corrections, start over, and try again from scratch. It is important that you do start over completely with a blank board. Once you get that concept down perfectly, move on to the next learning objective.

Self-Testing with Friends

In Chapter 6, I mentioned that notation reduction strategy was a powerful learning technique. I also mentioned that I like to review those cheat-sheets/cards to see how well students can recall lecture material from their cues.

Since professors cannot be available 24/7, you need to make some friends from class. Instead of the professor testing your mastery of course material, get your classmate to play that role. In this exercise, you get to use your cheat card while your friend uses his or her notes. If you cannot answer a question posed by your friend, you will discover gaps in your notecard. Remember, several days before the test, you will be down to a 3" x 5" cheat-card. It is important that you be tested several times before the exam.

From this learning check, you will discover what information you know really well and the information you do not know at all. And we know why that's vital. Precious study time can be devoted to the material you've not yet mastered.

Role Playing

Another technique I like using is the student-teacher dyad. Here, I team up two students from class who will eventually check each other's learning. I start by giving each student two clear learning objectives. After the students have mastered the learning objective, I assign one as the teacher, the other as the student. This way, both will be at a good level of mastery since the "student" actually serves as the person responsible for the learning check. The teacher's task is to teach the concept without using notes. The student follows the lecture using notes to check for errors. When a mistake is made, the teacher is alerted, and a correction is made. After that learning check is completed, they switch places and tackle the second topic.

But there is something more that happens in these student-teacher dyad study groups. Preparing for teaching and delivering a mini-lecture forces a student to process information at a much deeper level. This has real benefits for the teacher. For example, one study compared learning outcomes between students given a reading assignment to study versus another group of students given the same reading assignment who prepared to teach it to another group. The second group showed better exam performance (Bargh and Schul, 1980). The improvements were a full letter grade higher.

So ask yourself this question: **Would you rather pay for a tutor? Or be paid to tutor?** You see, it pays to be a tutor in more ways than one. Cash and grades.

The importance of self-testing or learning checks cannot be over-stated. Certainly, it makes you a more efficient learner by focusing valuable study time on material not well-learned, but there is a bigger effect. It turns out that this technique leads to better long-term retention of material than strategies without self-tests.

Professors Jeffrey Karpicke and Henry Roediger, III (2008) conducted an interesting study worth mentioning because the effects are so dramatic. Different groups of students were asked to learn forty word pairs (Swahili-English) using one of four study strategies — two of which included repeated testing over the entire list of word pairs while the other two strategies did not. While all four groups managed to reach perfect recall at the same rate during the learning phase of the study, there were remarkable differences in test performance one week later. The two groups who repeatedly self-tested all material during the learning phase correctly recalled 80% of the word pairs. The other two groups, one of which self-tested on only the incorrect word pairs during the learning phase, correctly recalled well under 40% of the pairs. Remember, all groups appeared to learn the material well during the initial learning sessions, but the ability to recall it a week later was dramatically affected. If I were assigning grades to those groups, they'd have Bs and Fs, respectively. So the key is —

"The importance of self-testing in studying cannot be overstated."

1. **Study all material using learning objectives.**
2. **Self-test to identify what you do and do not know.**
3. **Study only the material not yet mastered.**
4. **Repeat self-testing over all material.**

We learned in Rule 5 that spacing out your study times into more frequent, smaller sessions increases exam performance. And in Rule 6 we learned that creating concept maps also increases exam performance. In a recent experiment, Professors Karpicke and Blunt (2011) compared learning performance using those two study strategies against a self-testing strategy and found some pretty amazing results — especially on the higher levels of learning we discussed in Rule 7.

Karpicke and Blunt

These researchers took a group of eighty undergraduate students, had them all study a science text under one of four learning conditions. One group was given a single study session. A second group was given four consecutive study sessions (Rule #5). A third group was told to use study time constructing concept maps (Rule #6). Finally, a fourth group was given the same amount of time to study, but told to self-test (Rule #8). This group was allowed to study the text once more and perform a second self-test. One week later, the students returned to complete a short-answer test. The kind of test questions given on this quiz contained both factual- and conceptual-level type questions (remember Rule #7).

Not surprisingly, the repeated study, concept mapping and self-testing groups outperformed the single study session group. The proportion of correct answers in

"Go back to Rule #6 and find the penny exercise. Can you pick out the correct penny this time?

...Bet you can."

the single-study session group was an abysmal 28%. The proportion of correct responses in the second and third groups (repeated study and concept mapping) was just under 50%. Now that is a pretty big performance boost in itself. But here's where things get interesting. The proportion of correct answers in the self-testing group was nearly 70%.

That is a 50% boost in exam performance over the second and third groups! These increases in performance occurred in essentially one sitting, using pretty straightforward study strategies — self-testing. Imagine combining the techniques of spaced-out study sessions, concept mapping, and self-testing over a one or two week-long preparation period. That would get your A game on.

Self-testing is a game changer when it comes to improving test performance and is one of the hottest areas of study in cognitive psychology. Meta-analyses of data from over 100 studies show substantial improvement in testing outcomes using this study strategy (Adesope, Trevisan and Sundararajan, 2017). It not only focuses your learning on areas that need additional study; we now know that self-testing re-activates brain pathways that underlie memory, strengthens the connections that form these memories, and increases learning and test performance (Bonin and De Koninck, 2015). You should be able to walk into an exam and have a very good idea of how well you will perform on that exam. Why? If you follow Rule #8, you will have already tested yourself. If you are correctly recalling 95%–100% of the material during your multiple study sessions, you will leave that exam with an A. If your self-testing yields 85% correct, you have made it to the level of a B grade.

By the way, go back to Chapter 6 (page 37) and find the penny exercise. Can you pick out the correct penny this time? Bet you did. Use learning objectives and learning checks. These are key game changers in making you an A student.

Rule
#

Be Exam Savvy

A

Many years ago, I was visiting relatives in Minnesota. At one point, my young cousin expressed frustration about an upcoming important test. It was for her driver's license written exam. On the take-home practice test, she had missed too many questions to pass. I'd be frustrated too. Relying on your parents and others to provide taxi service for the rest of your life is a bit embarrassing.

I asked her to give me the practice test booklet. I was curious to see whether I could pass. I've never taken the Minnesota exam, but having passed my own state licensing exam and having been driving for more than forty years, I figured I could pull out a passing score. I read through the multiple-choice test, and sure enough, there were plenty of easy questions. There were harder ones — things like distance between vehicles and speed limits on certain roadways. And then there were even harder questions that referenced laws specific to Minnesota. It looked like I might actually have to study for this one.

But I know how to write multiple-choice exams. And when you do, you know how to avoid common exam-writing mistakes. These kinds of mistakes can help the savvy exam-taker like me earn better scores. I will tell you what tricks to use when taking a test to help narrow down a choice when you have no idea what to select. I used these principles to answer questions on the Minnesota driver's licensing exam. I passed. My cousin pulled up a chair for a lesson.

Deadly Habit(s)

The most common test-taking blunders include —
1) **not reading the question carefully;**
2) **attempting to answer each question in the order** presented, even when stuck;
3) making **scantron marking errors**; and
4) **forgetting to look on the back of the last page** for any exam questions.

Seriously on that last one: just last term a student did not answer the last eight questions on the final exam.

The Game Changer

The first thing to do is put your scantron down. You will fill that in after taking the exam. Go through the exam and answer all of the questions that you can answer instantly. If one hangs you up a bit, just move on. Oftentimes, a subsequent question will jog your memory. At that point, just go back and select the correct answer. Now if you have actually applied Rules #1-8 in earnest, you will be finished with the exam and will score an A. From here, just carefully transfer the correct answers to the scantron. Too many times, a student will have marked the correct answer on the test booklet, but will have failed to bubble in the same on the scantron. As a professor, what am I to do? As far as I know, you changed your mind on that item.

The Tough Questions

Let's assume there will be situations where you will have to go back through the exam to tackle one of those harder questions. What do you do now? Well, first thing to do is completely understand what the question is asking. You may want to reword the question. I generally do this by saying, "This question is asking me to … " Next is to scratch out choices that are obviously incorrect. We call those *foils* in the business of exam writing. Again, if you have done your work and encounter a term you've never seen, that is *not* the correct answer. Scratch it out. So how many are you down to? Two? Well, that is better than three or four. Just think about this. On a five-item multiple-choice question where you don't know the answer, you have a 20% chance of getting it correct. Get that down to three choices, and your odds go up to 33%. Eliminate one more foil, and now you have a 50% chance of getting it correct. Now here are some additional tips that should help.

Long Answers

In writing good multiple-choice questions, I teach my graduate students to be certain that the foils are the same length as the correct answer. If you see choices that vary in length and do not know the correct answer, pick the one that is the longest. Lazy instructors often don't put the time in writing foils. They are typically shorter. I followed this rule on that Minnesota driver's licensing exam and got all of those answers correct. This works only if your teacher does not know how to write exam questions.

Numbers

Another thing I teach future college professors is that when using numbers in answers, 1) order them from low-to-high or high-to-low for clarity and 2) be certain that the correct answer has an equal chance to appear in any position. While new teachers may put the numbers in order, they rarely place the correct answer in the lowest or highest spot. So if you happen to be stuck on this type question, throw out the high and low, and pick one in the middle. This raises your odds of getting a correct answer from 20%-25% to 33%-50%. I used this strategy on the Minnesota driver's licensing exam and got many of those questions correct. Remember, this works only if your teacher does not know how to write exam questions.

The same principle applies to locating the correct answer in the series of choices. The standard rule is that each choice a, b, c, d, and e should contain the correct answer roughly the same number of times throughout the test. Teachers tend to avoid placing the correct answers in the first and last location. When in doubt what to select on an exam, avoid choices a and e (or d if there are only four choices). Again, this works only if your teacher does not know how to write exam questions.

Typos

Here's a simple one. If one of the alternatives is not grammatically correct or contains a misspelling, it is not the correct answer. You see, teachers have a tendency to write the exam question first, write the correct answer next, and then write three or four foils. Sometimes the instructor runs out of steam and is a bit careless in writing those foils. They tend to proof the exam by scanning for only the correct answer and rarely for whether the foil is grammatically correct. I see this all the time, and it is a dead giveaway to avoid that foil (I sometimes catch one on my own exams!).

On Second Guessing

Students always ask me about whether to change an answer once they select one. The rule they tend to follow is to go with your first instinct. I agree, but I want to add another rule to that. The only times you change your answers are 1) you know that another alternative is absolutely correct, and 2) you know the choice you initially selected is absolutely wrong.

Now those rules seem obvious. But here is where students violate the rule. They start to second-guess themselves. They're not sure if they did select the correct answer. Or, they think that maybe another is a better choice. What they're feeling is a lack of confidence. So they change the answer. In either case they have violated the two rules I just mentioned. If you stick with those two rules, you are more likely to change an answer from incorrect to correct and avoid changing a correct answer to incorrect.

I admit to having some mixed feelings about revealing to you some of these tips in taking exams. At the same time, if instructors became better exam writers, none of these tips would apply except for the first (don't get yourself hung up on a question) and last (changing an answer) tips. And those two are worth keeping in your toolbox of tips to increasing exam performance.

Review your Exam

You may have noticed how much I can learn about a student's study habits and skills simply by looking over his or her exams. You can do the same thing. Think of this as your diagnostic check up in order to change your habits and strategies in prepping for the next test. Go see your professor to review your exam item by item. Are you starting too late in studying (Rule #5)? That will show as better performance on the first half of the exam than the second. Are you missing questions because you do not have any lecture notes on that content? You must have been distracted by something in lecture that day (Rule #2). Are you getting only the factual questions correct? Then you're violating Rule #7. Could you narrow some questions down to two or three choices but ended up missing it? Then you did not self-test well enough (Rule #8).

Yet Another Game Changer

Now I have something to say to those of you who suffer from test anxiety that results in horrible exam performance. There's hope! A great study published by Professors Gerardo Ramirez and Sian Beilock (2011) from the University of Chicago shows that a simple ten-minute exercise can, in fact, boost test scores in students who "choke under pressure" in high-stakes testing.

The idea behind this approach is that high-stakes testing, where you have large incentives for excellent scores (e.g., high GPAs, scholarships, job opportunities) and large negative consequences for poor scores (e.g., returning to your old high school job of flipping burgers or serving lattes), causes students to worry and become anxious.

Excessive worrying competes with the limited resources of your working memory. And working memory is the part of our information-processing system that allows us to maintain focus, and access and work with information relevant to ongoing tasks. It follows that if your working memory is taxed with excessive worries about test performance, there will be fewer cognitive resources devoted to exam-taking. The question is, then, how do we best free the working memory from such destructive rumination?

The process is a simple ten-minute expressive writing exercise that is completed immediately before the exam. The task: write as openly as possible about your thoughts and feelings regarding the test. Given that the exam is just around the corner, there should be much to express in that ten-minute period.

The Ramirez & Beilock study used a pre-test/post-test in which students solved math problems. However, the second math test was a high-stakes test. The student was told that an excellent team score, which was now totally in their hands, led to a large monetary reward. Prior to the second test, one group sat quietly for ten minutes (control group) while another group engaged in the ten-minute expressive writing exercise (experimental group). Both groups then took the high-stakes post-test.

Math scores on the pre-test were not different from one another. However, students in the control group showed a 12% decline in their test performance. Students in the expressive writing group showed a 5% increase in their test scores. That change in performance from having test anxiety and choking to overcoming test anxiety (and not choking) is a one-and-a-half letter grade difference. Remarkable.

A follow-up study found the same pattern. But it also found that the biggest boost in exam scores came from students whose writing expressed more negative thoughts and emotions.

So the key here is to ensure you are writing about your worries rather than about something unrelated to the upcoming exam.

It is amazing how detrimental test anxiety can be on test performance and how beneficial an expressive writing exercise can be on boosting test outcomes.

So if you suffer the debilitating effects of test anxiety, find a quiet spot in the lobby or library just before the exam and spend ten minutes writing about those test anxieties. Never show it to anyone. Get your fears and anxieties out of your head and onto the paper. Drop it in the trash on your way to the exam.

It is one more way to get into your A game.

The Difference Between
Can't and **Won't**

Epilogue

A

Here's a conversation I overheard.

One of Professor Wilson's students was lamenting her poor class performance.

"Any chance you could have done better?" Professor Wilson asked.

"I don't think so," she said. "I tried everything."

"What was the hardest class you've ever taken?" Professor Wilson asked the student.

"Definitely Dr. Sufka's brain and behavior course," she answered. "No doubt about it."

"Oh yeah," Professor Wilson said, "that is a tough one. Lots of new words and concepts. His lectures sound like they're in a foreign language." Professor Wilson thought for a moment. Then he asked, "What was your final grade in the class?"

"A 'D'," the student told him.

"So ... " Professor Wilson said, "there was nothing you could have done in that brain class to get a C?"

"No," she said. "I gave it everything I had ... and feel lucky I didn't get an F."

Professor Wilson then asked, "Do you love your mother?"

"What?" the student asked, a bit taken aback.

"Your mother," he clarified. "Do you love her?"

"Uh ... yes," the student said.

"Do you really love her?" he pushed.

"Of course," she said, "I love my mother."

"OK, then," Professor Wilson said, "I've kidnapped your mother, and I am holding a gun to her head."

At this point I lean forward over my desk to peer inside Professor Wilson's office. He has one arm cradled as if clutching an imaginary person in a head-lock and is holding his free hand into the shape of a weapon with a two-finger gun barrel pointed toward her head. I'm thinking he has lost his mind. I am sure the student has similar thoughts.

Then Professor Wilson said to her, "Are you telling me that you could not do anything to get a better grade in Sufka's class? If your mother's life depended on your getting a C, could you have done it?"

The student was speechless.

"C'mon," Professor Wilson taunted, "better grade or your mother's life? Which will it be?"

"Well," she answered, "I suppose I could have gotten a better grade."

"Suppose!?" Professor Wilson said, "Your mother's life depends on it."

" Well," she said, "then yes, I could have."

"What would have you done to get a better grade?" he asked.

"I'm not sure."

"C'mon," he said. "I've still got your momma."

Eventually Professor Wilson prodded the student along until she listed, among others: attend every class, record lectures, spend more study time, get a tutor, and meet with the professor.

• • •

Here was Professor Wilson's main point. **There is a big difference between can't and won't.** The student in Professor Wilson's office shifted from *can't* get a better grade to *won't* do what is necessary to get a better grade. This is an extraordinary change in worldview — going from being powerless to being fully in control of the outcome in your life. As the student left his office, Professor Wilson offered one last word of encouragement, "Now don't make me shoot your momma!"

I believe in my students, and I let them know. I believe you are capable of accomplishing any goal if you put your mind, heart, and soul to the task. Mastering strategic learning skills and getting A grades can be a challenge to many students. But these goals are attainable. Trust me.

And believe in yourself.

Do all of my students who receive this advice go on to success in college? Sadly, no. Why? I can only assume they did not want to put in the effort. I suppose there were other things more important in their lives.

But those students who do follow through with my advice see measurable changes in their grades.

I remember one student, Brian, who many years ago took my general psychology class. As a freshman, he stopped by my office after a poor performance on the first exam. I went through my diagnostic check-list and gave him the same set of strategic learning tips given to you in this book. Sure enough, he scored an A on the second test. He continued to earn As for the next three exams. At the end of the term, just before heading home for winter recess, he stopped by to thank me. Having not given much thought to our discussion of strategic learning tips months earlier, I asked, "For what?"

He said I completely changed the way he prepped for classes and exams. He added that he had pulled out a 4.0 GPA for the term.

He applied what he learned to each of his courses. That gave me a reason to smile.

Another semester passed, and Brian stopped by my office again. I remembered him from the previous semester, and he wanted to thank me again because he had pulled off another semester of excellent grades. On top of that, he told me he now had much more free time on his hands. He had stopped wasting time studying in inefficient ways.

I saw Brian a few years later. He was sitting in a lecture hall where I was to give a presentation. The topic was "Getting Students to Become Strategic Learners." I was presenting to 150 graduate students who had been assigned to teach undergraduate courses. Midway through the presentation, I looked at Brian, and we shared a smile. He has done well.

Take this advice to heart and I am sure you will, too. Good luck.

<u>A</u>

References

Adesope, O.O., Trevisan, D.A. and Sundararajan, N. (2017). "Rethinking the use of tests: A meta-analysis of practice testing." *Review of Educational Research*, Vol. 87, pp. 659-701.

Bargh, J.A. and Schul, Y.(1980). "On the cognitive benefits of teaching." *Journal of Educational Psychology*, Vol. 72, pp. 593-604.

Benedict, M. and Hoag, J. (2004). "Seating location in large lectures: Is location related to performance?" *Journal of Economics Education*, Vol. 35, pp. 215-231.

Berry J.W. and Chew, S.L. (2008). "Improving learning through interventions of student-generated questions and concept maps." *Teaching of Psychology*, Vol. 35, pp. 305-312.

Bloom, B.S. (1956). *Taxonomy of educational objectives: The classification of educational goals*. New York: Longman, Green.

Bloom, B. Mesia, B. and Krathwohl, D. (1964). *Taxonomy of Educational Objectives (The Affective Domain and The Cognitive Domain)*. New York: David McKay.

Bonin, R.P. and De Koninck, Y. (2015). "Reconsolidation and the regulation of plasticity: Moving beyond memory." *Trends in Neuroscience*, Vol. 38, pp. 336-344.

Chan, J.C.K., McDermott, K.B. and Roediger III, H.L. (2006). "Retrieval-induced facilitation: Initially nontested material can benefit from prior testing of related material." *Journal of Experimental Psychology: General*, Vol. 135, pp. 553–571.

Dietz-Uhler, B. and Lanter, J.R. (2009). "Using the four-question technique to enhance learning." *Teaching of Psychology*, Vol. 36, pp. 38-41.

Donovan, J.J. and Radosevich, D.J. (1999). "A meta-analytic review of the distribution of practice effect: Now you see it, now you don't." *Journal of Applied Psychology*, Vol. 84, pp. 795-805.

Dunlosky, J., Rawson, K.A., Marsh, E.J., Nathan, M. J. and Willingham, D.T. (2013). "Improving students' learning with effective learning techniques: Promising directions from cognitive and educational psychology." *Psychological Science in the Public Interest*, Vol. 14, pp. 4-58.

Gingerich A.C. and Lineweaver T.T. (2014). "OMG! Texting in class = U fail :(empirical evidence that text messaging during class disrupts comprehension." *Teaching of Psychology*, Vol. 41, pp. 44-51.

Karpicke, J.D. and Blunt, J.R. (2011). "Retrieval practice produces more learning than elaborative studying with concept mapping." *Science*, Vol. 331, pp. 772-775.

Karpicke, J.D. and Roediger III, H.L. (2008). "The critical importance of retrieval for learning." *Science*, Vol. 319, pp. 966-968.

Marshall, P.D. and Losonczy-Marshall, M. (2010). "Classroom ecology: Relations between seating location, performance and attendance." *Psychological Reports*, Vol. 107, pp. 557-577.

Mueller, P.A. and Oppenheimer, D. M. (2014). "The pen is mightier than the keyboard: Advantages of longhand over laptop note taking." *Psychological Science*, Vol. 25, pp.1159-1168.

Nesbit, J.C. and Adesope, O.O. (2006). "Learning with concept and knowledge maps: A meta-analysis." *Review of Educational Research*, Vol. 76, pp. 413-448.

Ramirez, G. and Beilock S.L. (2011). "Writing about testing worries boosts exam performance in the classroom." *Science*, Vol. 331, pp. 211-213.

Williamson, E.G (1935). "The relationship of number of hours of study to scholarship." *Journal of Educational Psychology*, Vol. 26(9), pp. 682-688.

Acknowledgements

I thank the University of Mississippi for providing sabbatical opportunities to write both editions of *The A Game*. Many thanks to my students for reaching out for help and in trusting my advice in mastering course material. Without these conversations, this study guide would have never come to life. I am grateful for the many conversations with my friend and colleague Professor Kelly Wilson, who shares my passion for teaching and mentoring. Many thanks to my editor, Neil White, for bringing clarity and coherence to my writing, and to the entire team at Nautilus Publishing in their support to promote student academic success. Finally, I thank my entire family for their love and support.

About the Author

Dr. Kenneth Sufka joined the University of Mississippi faculty in 1992 after earning a Ph.D. in physiological psychology from Iowa State University. He is a professor of psychology with joint appointments in pharmacology, philosophy and the Research Institute of Pharmaceutical Sciences. He is a best selling-author and sought-after speaker at colleges and universities across the United States on the topic of evidenced-based student academic success.

His laboratory research interests cover a range of topics in neuroscience, pharmacology, and philosophy of mind. He has published more than eighty research articles and chapters in these areas. His main expertise is the development, validation, and utilization of animal models and procedures to enhance translational relevance in drug discovery, focusing mainly on chronic pain and analgesia and stress-related disorders.

Dr. Sufka regularly teaches general psychology and brain and behavior, among other courses. He has received numerous recognitions during his career at Ole Miss, including the University of Mississippi's Elsie M. Hood Outstanding Teaching Award in 1996, the University of Mississippi's Faculty Achievement Award for Outstanding Teaching and Scholarship in 2005, and the school's Thomas F. Frist Student Service in 2006.

Dr. Sufka has also been recognized by the American Psychological Association's Presidential Citation for his national-level efforts at undergraduate curricular reform and by Iowa State University Department of Psychology's Alumni Achievement Award for exceptional contributions to teaching and service to the profession and community. In 2014, he received a prestigious national teaching recognition by being named Mississippi's CASE-Carnegie U.S. Professor of the Year.

In his free time, Dr. Sufka enjoys designing and building furniture in his woodshop and taking cross-country road trips on his Harley-Davidson and BMW motorcycles.